GW00771676

Lorrie Tallis

Wells-next-the-Sea
People & Places

A photographic portrait of a Norfolk coastal town
in the first decade of the twenty-first century

Janet Angles & John Warham

Dedication

To Paul, Jane, Katie, Jane and Greg

First Published 2010

ISBN 978-0-9553333-3-0

A catalogue record for this book is available from the British Library.

Designed by Dick Malt

Published by Thornham Local History Society
Red Brick House
Hall Lane
Thornham
Norfolk
PE36 6NB

Printed by Dolphin Graphics
Dersingham, Norfolk

Contents

Introduction

In 2009, I completed *Thornham – People & Places*, an attempt to portray the village in which I live during the first decade of the twenty-first century. The idea of doing a similar book on the much larger town of Wells was given to me by Catherine Edgington of Big Blue Sky, who, when taking some of my Thornham books to sell, asked, 'what are you going to do next, how about a book on Wells?' I could see that the format of the book could apply equally to Wells, but, though I thought I could manage the shots of the 'Places' involved, I felt I would not adequately be able to cover the 'People' aspect. I then had the inspiration of asking Janet Angles, whom I have known through studying digital photography together at Wells Library, if she would like to join me in the project. Janet welcomed the opportunity and, having lived in Wells for ten years, was quickly contacting her friends and acquaintances and providing some of the photos you see in these pages.

We were fortunate to meet up with Mike Welland at an early stage in the process. Mike and the publications of the Wells Local History Group provided an invaluable guide to how the town has developed over the centuries and, we hope, provided a backcloth against which to portray Wells as it now is.

Wells at the end of the first decade of the twenty-first century is a busy town with many varied interests and activities represented, some of which we have tried to illustrate. Firmly established on the tourist map and thronged with visitors throughout the summer season, it is also a vibrant community with year-round activities for all. There is a library, theatre, hospital, secondary school, sailing club, tennis, bowls and croquet and much more. The fishing fleets and the railway of yesteryear may have gone but new activities trades, arts and crafts continue to flourish. Unfortunately, due to limitations of space, we have not been able to show all the crafts and activities which take place in the town, but hopefully we have provided a balanced view of the town as it is today.

All the photographs in this book, except where especially mentioned, were taken in Wells during 2009 and 2010 and represent a snapshot portrait of the town at the end of the first decade of a new millennium.

The Town Sign

The town sign stands at the top of Two Furlong Hill.

The original sign (right) was replaced by the anchor design in 2002 to celebrate the Golden Jubilee of the Queen. The new sign was designed by Cassie Turton and carved by Warren Trett.

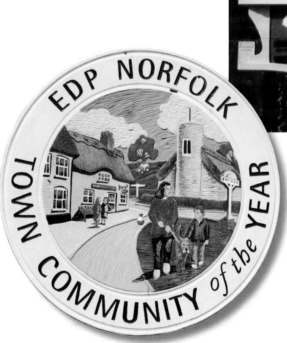

Wells was the winner of the *Eastern Daily Press* Town Community of the Year competition in 2005 and runner up in 2007. The sign (left), next to the Tourist Information Centre at the bottom of Staithe Street, celebrates this achievement.

A panoramic view of the harbour and quayside at high tide, taken from the East End.

Fish & Chips

Fish 'n' chips, the great British institution, is well represented on the Quayside. French's and Platten's do brisk business throughout the year and one of the most popular places to sit and eat is the quayside wall opposite.

Crabbing

Crabbing, or 'gillying', as it is known locally, has been a popular pastime with youngsters for generations. How often does the same old crab get hauled out of the water! As with most things, it now seems to have become more sophisticated than ever.

Amusement arcades

Amusement arcades – past and present. Hopefully the burnt out and boarded up Quayside buildings will soon be restored to life.

The *Albatros*

The *Albatros*, a Dutch clipper, was built in 1899 in Capelle near Rotterdam. She is a gaff-rigged ketch carrying eight sails. Originally built for Captain Johan Muller, she carried cargo between Holland and the Baltic ports for many years, surviving the First World War intact.

In 1920 she was sold to Captain Lolk of Denmark and in 1933 was fitted with her first engine. In 1941 she changed hands again, this time to Captain Rasmussen of Denmark and between 1941 and 1945 she carried Jews and political dissidents from Denmark to Sweden (a neutral country) returning to Denmark with guns hidden among the cargo for the Danish resistance. In 1964, Rasmussen altered the arrangement of her sails and fitted her with a bigger engine to continue carrying cargo until 1978 when he retired and she was laid up in Copenhagen.

Captain Ton Brouwer, her present owner, bought her in 1980 and sailed to Amsterdam to undergo a complete restoration. In 1987 she was again carrying cargo and was the last cargo ship under sail in Europe, working in the North Sea and the Baltic. She also used the experience of being at sea to help disaffected young people, who worked as crew and she sailed around 2,000 nautical miles each year.

Between 1990 and 1996 she became a regular visitor to Wells, bringing in over a hundred cargoes of soya meal from the continent to be used as cattle feed. From 1978 to 1998 after further refurbishing she was used as a passenger ship. From 1998 to 2000 she was chartered by Greenpeace and later used as a waterborne venue for children's education.

Since then, she has been based in Wells and is available for charter as well as for bed & breakfast and Dutch Pancakes, often with jazz or other musical accompaniment, in the evenings.

Traditional
DUTCH PANCAKES
Albatros
tel 07979 087228

- café restaurant
- licensed bar
- bed & breakfast
- live music

ALBATROS GALLEY MENU
SWEET PANCAKES (King Size):
- Lemon & sugar £3.50
- Cinnamon & maple syrup 3.75
- Jam, cinnamon & maple syrup ... 4.50
- Apple, cinnamon & syrup 5.25
- Chocolate & double cream 5.50
- Mincemeat & maple syrup 5.75
- Pear, Advokaat, whipped cream . 6.50

Savoury Pancake Meals:
- Cheese & baked beans £4.50
- Bacon & baked beans 5.50
- Mushroom, garlic & stilton 6.60
- Cheese, spinach & boiled egg 6.85
- Salami, mozzarella & tomato 6.95
- Ham, cheese & pineapple 6.95
- Smoked salmon, cream cheese, dill . 7.50

SEAFARER'S BRUNCH:
2-3 fried eggs on toast or bread
topped with either — cheese £4.95
— ham 5.25
or ham & cheese 5.95

KIDDIE'S PANCAKES £1.00 less

TODAY'S SPECIALS
Dutch Omelettes
served with bread, butter & salad
filled with cheese, ham, mush-
rooms or salmon from £5.50
MUSSELS
Brancaster Mussels
in a traditional Dutch
white wine sauce, bread &
£6.50 butter
CAKES
- VICTORIA SPONGE £2.25
- CHOCOLATE SPONGE £2.25
- £2.75

ALBATROS SPECIALS
Homemade Dutch pea soup
with ham/cheese roll £4.75
New pancakes:
- Sweet & spicy stem ginger,
ginger preserve, cinnamon syrup £6.50
- banana, cinnamon syrup & whipped
cream £5.75
HOT DRINKS:
- hot chocolate & Bailey's £2.50
- horlicks & Amaretto £2.50
- mulled wine £2.50
Dutch Bar Snack
(diced cheese, salami, gherkin & olives) £6.50

OPEN

Between decks on the *Albatros*, probably the only sailing
ship to appear in the annual CAMRA *Good Beer Guide*.

The Quay

Roughly a century separates these two pictures of the Quayside
but the view is still instantly recognizable.

Blucher

Andy McCullum built
Blucher together
with David Hewitt, a
friend from Blakeney.
He named it after his
grandfather, Ernie
Jarvis, whose nickname
was 'Blucher'.

NO PARKING
AT ANY TIME
ACCESS REQUIRED
24 HOURS FOR
BOAT LAUNCHING

BY ORDER OF WELLS HARBOUR COMMISSIONER

WARNING NOTICE
DANGER
WORKING QUAY
MOORING RINGS,
CHAINS, ROPES &
UNEVEN SURFACE
TAKE CARE

PRIVATE
LAND AND
QUAY.
KEEP OFF.

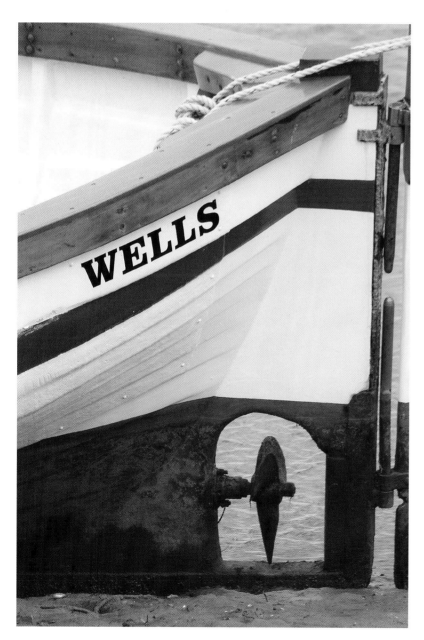

Allen Frary digging for bait early one bright winter morning.

Charles William being unloaded. Nicky King, the boat's owner, is aboard handing up the boxes of crabs, assisted by John Nudds and Bernie Tuck on the quay.

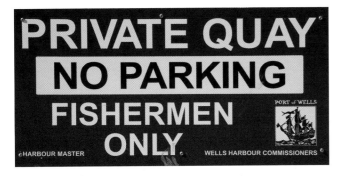

Fishing

After the second World War, there were only five or six fishing boats going out from Wells to catch whelks. They were all owned by Wells families: the Grimes; the Coxes; the Coopers; the Neilsons and the Peggs. The whelk beds were carefully managed and were used in rotation so that the whelks had time to spawn before being fished again.

In this way there were always plenty available and the boats were able to make a living. The fishermen also had mussel lays along the channel in the east end, rented from the Harbour Commissioners. The mussels were bought as seed and laid on mud to allow them to grow. The mussel lays have now gone as the channel is too sandy. During the winter the fishermen would spend time in maintaining the whelk pots and making new fishing nets.

The arrival of more boats in Wells led to overfishing. The whelk stocks dwindled and whelk fishing was abandoned by 1998.

The fishermen now put out pots to catch crabs and lobsters.

The Whelk Sheds

Until recently, boats would land whelks in net bags for boiling and bagging before being shipped out by road. These days the boiling process is carried out elsewhere and other uses are being found for the old sheds.

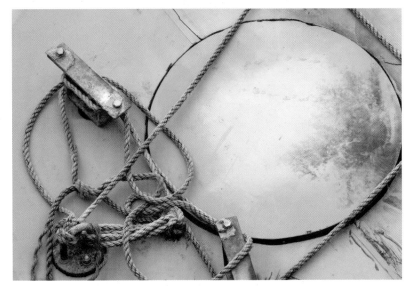

The Gantry

The Granary was built in 1906 as a warehouse for storing grain prior to loading on to ships in the harbour below via the gantry. It was converted into flats and offices in 1996.

In 2010, a new processing shed was opened on the quay (above, next to the lorry with the white cab). It is fitted with chillers and fridges and is primarily used for velvet crabs which are in great demand on the continent. It is also used for brown crabs, for storing bait and anything else that is required.

Looking past the chandlery to the East End with its fishermen's cottages and narrow streets and alleys, down to the sailing club and whelk sheds in the distance.

These spectacular and unusual 'birds eye' views of the harbour and Quayside were taken from Mr & Mrs Ian Scott's flat at the top of the Gantry.

Wells Tide Recorder Station

The tide recorder gauge was built in the early 1950s and recorded the heights of each high tide. Inside the building was a type of well which was fed by a water pipe from the harbour, and the water within it rose and fell with each tide. It has not been in use for a few years as the tide measurements are now recorded by computer.

Very high tides overtop the Quay, and the Wells sluice (below) is designed to keep the North Sea at bay! It is a sliding barrier costing much less than the Thames barrage but having the same objective in mind.

Wells Tide Recorder Station

WILDFOWLING

TAKES PLACE
ON THIS SEABANK

1st NOVEMBER-20TH FEBRUARY

HOLKHAM ESTATE
WELLS & DISTRICT WILDFOWLING CLUB

The Bank

Built in the 1850s to reclaim a large area of saltmarsh to the west as
agricultural land for the Holkham estate.

ROBERT WILLIAM
ELSDON.
(COXSWAIN)

The Eliza Adams Memorial

Built in 1906, the Lifeboat memorial commemorates the disaster of the Eliza Adams when eleven of the crew were drowned in an abortive rescue attempt.

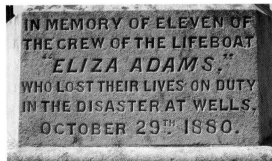

IN MEMORY OF ELEVEN OF THE CREW OF THE LIFEBOAT "ELIZA ADAMS." WHO LOST THEIR LIVES ON DUTY IN THE DISASTER AT WELLS. OCTOBER 29TH 1880.

New Harbour

Development of the Sheringham Shoal wind farm is bringing changes to the waterfront. A new outer harbour is being built and a deeper channel has been dredged to allow virtually twenty-four hour access to the wind farm twenty miles offshore. A central office with an information centre has opened on Staithe Street.

Marina

The marina, meanwhile, caters for smaller vessels and more recreational sailing.

48

STAITHE STREET NR23

You can buy just about anything along busy Staithe Street. These pictures show shop owners Mel Catton (right) and (overleaf) Hazel Ashley, Molly Caslow, Tracey Catton, Kerry & Mandy Dalton, Arthur Howell and Jules Jackson with their respective shops.

The Wells Flower Co.

WE SELL CRAB BAIT

CRAB BAIT
CRAB LINES
CRAB BUCKETS

MR. C's

SeaSail

85¢

1.49

5¢

LEATHER FOOTBALL
BASKETBALL
LARGE TENNIS BALL
SMALL FOOTBALL
GLITTER BALL
PLASTIC FOOTBALL
SPIKEY BALL

ARTHUR HOWELL BAKERY

NORMAL for NORFOLK

The Picnic Hut

The Wells Flower Co.

WELLS CLUB
Live FOOTBALL on
on the BIG Screen
TEMPORARY MEMBERSHIP
NOW AVAILABLE £1 a day
£5 a week £10 a fortnight.
FAMILY ROOM.
OPEN 4:30 FRIDAYS

Molly's

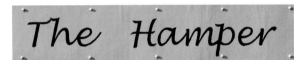
The Hamper

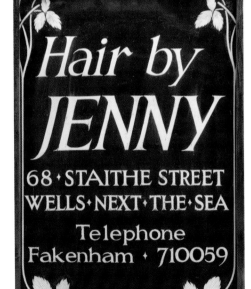
Hair by
JENNY

68 · STAITHE STREET
WELLS · NEXT · THE · SEA

Telephone
Fakenham · 710059

Phoebe's

Country Garden

GOLDING'S

Bean 2 the Coast
COFFEE HOUSE

MR . C's

SEAFOOD

CRAZY
CLEARANCE
UPSTAIRS

SHORT
N
CURLY
DOG
SALON
TEL 710725

NOW
OPEN
UPSTAIRS
LOTS OF
FRAMES
MIRRORS
PRESENT BAGS
GIFT WRAP
CARDS &
PHOTO ALBUMS

GOOD
PRICES!
MENS
& LADIES
SOCKS &
UNDERWEAR
ETC.

The Granary

The former granary and maltings was built in the nineteenth century and is now managed by the Wells Community Association. It is the venue for many group activities, as well as Wells Town Council Meetings.

High Street

In the nineteenth century High Street had more than forty shops and was the commercial centre of Wells. With the growing emergence of Staithe Street it waned in importance and is now a quiet residential street – here is a selection of the buildings.

The many faces of the brightly painted frontages of the former shops, now mainly residential houses, in High Street.

Left: Once the King's Arms pub, now Wells Tandoori.

Right: One of the two ostler's cottages either side of the gateway which led to the rear entrance of a former pub. The ostler's job was to look after horses for the night when travellers lodged in the inn.

Terraced cottages on the north side of Freeman Street dating from 1825 include, on the right hand side, the former Sailors' Home public house.

Left: One of Well's few remaining timber-framed houses, probably built in the fifteenth century, is in a yard off Freeman Street, and is now a B&B.

Right: New houses and flats at the western end of Freeman Street.

68

What's on in Wells this week?

THE BUTTLANDS

Most of the houses in this panorama (above) of the Buttlands were built by Samuel Fox in the 1830s. Samuel owned the ropewalk running at the back of the houses. Sadly, he went bankrupt.

The Enclosure Act stipulated that this was the only land in the parish that could not be enclosed. The original meaning of Buttlands was probably waste ground.

72

GREEN DRAGON LANE

TWO FURLONG HILL

 GREAT EASTERN WAY

KNITTING NEEDLE LANE

LEADING TO
HONEYMOON ROW NR23

THEATRE ROAD NR23

POLKA ROAD NR23

PARISH OF WELLS-NEXT-THE-SEA
WARHAM ROAD NR23

QUAYSIDE
COTTAGE

WHALEBONE YARD

PLEASE
DO NOT FEED
HORSES

NO DOGS
NO ALCOHOL
NO CYCLING
By order of Wells Town Council.

1819

GUELLA
HOUSE

CHADD
HOUSE

GOODWIN
COTTAGES

LIARS
CORNER

This old town pump is just off Church Plain by the side of St Nicholas' Church. It stands on the site of an old well.

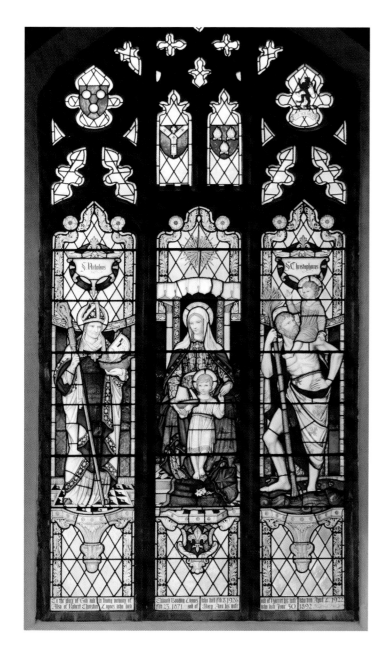

St Nicholas Church

Built in the fifteenth century on the site of an earlier church. Much of the present church was destroyed by a fire caused by a strike of lightning in 1879. It was rebuilt and consecrated again in 1883.

IN MEMORY OF, AND THANKSGIVING FOR
THE LIFE AND WORK OF
EDWARD BUNTING LOYNES,
CHURCHWARDEN OF THIS CHURCH OF St NICHOLAS
FOR 54 YEARS.
"SAFE HOME, SAFE HOME IN PORT"
R·I·P

78

Bell ringers Jean Terrington, Diane Walker, Peter Terrington
and Jeremy Gash.

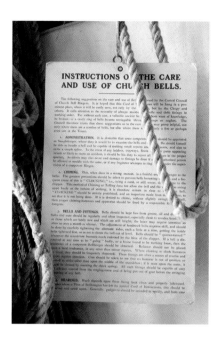

NORWICH DIOCESAN ASSOCIATION
OF
RINGERS
ON SATURDAY
JULY 18TH 1903
A PEAL OF BOB MAJOR
5008 CHANCES IN 3 5
TENOR 18CWT

J. SKINNER (WELLS) TREBLE
F. WILLIAMSON (WELLS) 2
W. HENDRY (WELLS) 3
C. AYERS (N. ELMHAM) 4
W. SAVORY (WELLS) 5
H. ELLIS (WELLS) 6
W. BURROWS (N. ELMHAM) 7
W. HOWSON (N. ELMHAM) TENOR
W. HOWSON CONDUCTOR

J. LOYNES } CHURCHWARDENS
E. B. LOYNES }
REV. C. H. N. INGLE. M. A. RECTOR

The Bell RIngers of St. Nicholas meet regularly for practice on Tuesday evenings under the leadership of the Tower Captain, Suzanne Rands. New members are always welcome to cover the many occasions on which the bells are rung.

The peal board (above right) records the occasion when all eight bells were rung in a sequence without any repetitions in the combination of the bells. This took about three hours to complete, so a quarter peal is usually rung for special events such as the start of the August carnival week, the Coronation and the Millennium.

The Evangelical Congregational Church

Originally built in 1817 and closed for many years before reopening for services in 1992.

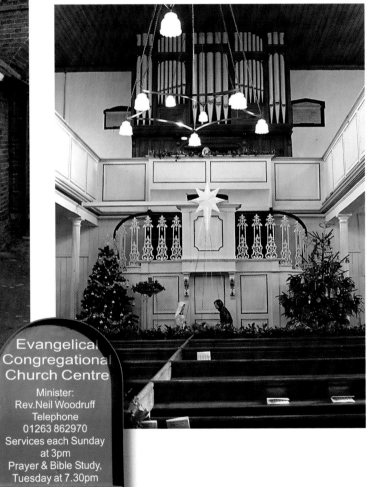

Evangelical Congregational Church Centre
Minister:
Rev.Neil Woodruff
Telephone
01263 862970
Services each Sunday
at 3pm
Prayer & Bible Study,
Tuesday at 7.30pm

The Salvation Army

Every week, Graham Green is in Wells collecting donations for the Salvation Army and handing out copies of the 'War Cry' magazine. Graham became a soldier in the Salvation Army around 30 years ago while living in Grimsby and, now in his 80s, he travels to Fakenham on Thursdays and Wells on Fridays from his home in Burnham Market to help to spread the message of the Salvation Army.

The Society of Friends

The Society of Friends (Quakers) first bought a house and land in Wells in 1697. The original buildings have been developed over the years.

The Methodist Chapel

Built in 1891 as a replacement for the earlier chapel
in Chapel Yard. Refurbished in 1991.

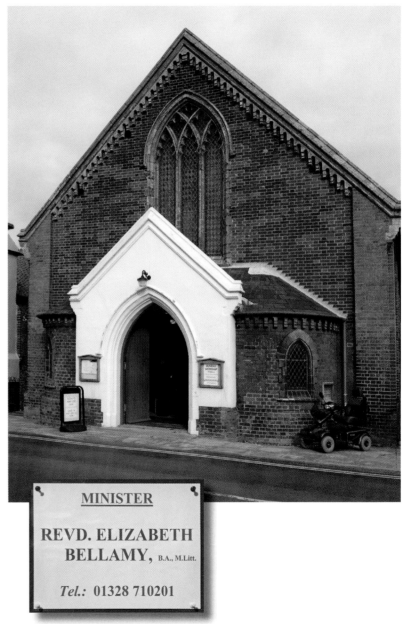

MINISTER

REVD. ELIZABETH
BELLAMY, B.A., M.Litt.

Tel.: 01328 710201

Church of Our Lady Star of the Sea

Consecrated in 1928, the church was paid for anonymously by Louis Cafferata of Stiffkey Old Hall. His gift was revealed in 1941 after his death.

The Golden Fleece

The Golden Fleece is one of the oldest public houses in Wells and its upper meeting room was the centre of many town activities including meetings of the Magistrates' Courts until this role was taken over by the Crown on the Buttlands.

The plaster reliefs (pictured here) date from the early eighteenth century and are thought to be of Flemish origin. They illustrate the importance of the woollen industry and sea faring to the local economy.

The Globe

The Globe has recently been refurbished by its owners, the Holkham Estate, and is managed by Adnams Brewery.

The Crown

The Crown began trading on the Buttlands in 1831 and took over from The Fleece on the Quay as the centre of social and civic activity in the town. Even the visiting dentist had a weekly surgery here.

The Crown is now part of the local Flying Kiwi chain of pubs/ restaurants run by New Zealander, Chris Coubrough and his team.

The Ark Royal

The Ark Royal reflects the style of the late 1960s period in which it was built. There is a small market held in the car park on Sunday mornings.

The Bowling Green

The Bowling Green no longer has a bowling green, but still has very much of a local feel about it. The pub is, as with so many other pubs throughout the country, immediately opposite the parish church and is one of the oldest in town. It has been in continuous operation for some 350 years.

The Edinburgh

The Edinburgh has, like so many of the other pubs in town, seen many changes of name since it first opened for business. It was originally known as the Fighting Cocks – perhaps it was a venue for cock fighting – before becoming the Leicester Arms. It is the meeting place of the Wells Lions.

88

This was the
KINGS
ARMS
PUBLIC HOUSE
c1832-1910
Wells Local History Group

This was the
LEICESTER
ARMS
PUBLIC HOUSE
1842-1888
Wells Local History Group

This was the
FIGHTING
COCKS
PUBLIC HOUSE
c1750-1842
Wells Local History Group

This was the
THREE
SWANS
PUBLIC HOUSE
c1720-1750
Wells Local History Group

This was the
DUKES
HEAD
PUBLIC HOUSE
c1750-1780
Wells Local History Group

This is the site of the
NORFOLK
FREEHOLDERS
PUBLIC HOUSE
c1835-1904
Wells Local History Group

This house was
THE
HOLKHAM
ARMS
PUBLIC HOUSE
c1832-1895
Wells Local History Group

This was the
JOLLY SAILOR
PUBLIC HOUSE
1807-1904
Wells Local History Group

This was the
EIGHT
RINGERS
PUBLIC HOUSE
c1780-c1970
Wells Local History Group

This was the
RAILWAY
HOTEL
1846-1964
Wells Local History Group

This was
THE
GRAPES
PUBLIC HOUSE
1835-1890
Wells Local History Group

This was
THE
SUN
PUBLIC HOUSE
c1750-1920
Wells Local History Group

This is the site of the
ANCHOR
PUBLIC HOUSE
c1881-1896
Wells Local History Group

This was the
SAILORS HOME
PUBLIC HOUSE
1851-1897
Wells Local History Group

This was the
TEWKSBURY ARMS
PUBLIC HOUSE
c1870-1888
Wells Local History Group

This was the
PARK TAVERN
PUBLIC HOUSE
1863-1975
Wells Local History Group

EXCHANGE
PUBLIC HOUSE
1835-1883
Wells Local History Group

This building was the
CROWN & ANCHOR
PUBLIC HOUSE
1798-1856
Wells Local History Group

This was the
SHIP INN
c1805-1960
Wells Local History Group

This was the
GREEN DRAGON
PUBLIC HOUSE
c1750-1865
Wells Local History Group

Wells Local History Group

These plaques were made at Wells Pottery and painted by Janet Birkett, a member of the Local History Group. They can be found on many of the historic buildings – most seem to have been pubs!

This was the
POST OFFICE
c1815-1851
Postmistress
Hannah Southgate
Wells Local History Group

This was the
POST OFFICE
1851-1912
Postmasters
John Southgate 1851-62
Francis Southgate 62-96
Jane Southgate
1896-1912
Wells Local History Group

JOHN FRYER R.N.
1753-1817
LIVED HERE
Sailing Master
'BOUNTY'
Wells Local History Group

90

The Old Railway Station

Wells Station was opened in 1857 by the Wells & Fakenham Railway which, from 1862, became part of the Great Eastern Railway's Wymondham to Wells branch. In 1866 a junction opened to the West Norfolk Junction Railway from Hunstanton.

The North Sea flood of 1953 so severely damaged the track between Wells and Holkham that the line between them was closed permanently. All the remaining lines were closed in 1964 as part of the Beeching Plan.

The station now houses the Pottery and Bookshop.

The Library

The town library was formerly a nineteenth-century Wesleyan chapel while the adjoining building (right) was the home of the Fire Service until 1965.

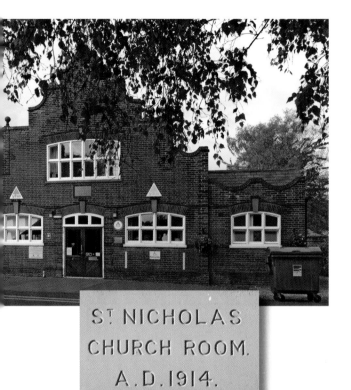

The Post Office

The Post Office and the Field Study Centre, formerly the school (below), show the range of local building materials from carrstone in the post office to flint cobbles and Holkham brick in the former school.

The Field Study Centre

The Youth Hostel

The Youth Hostel is housed in what used to be the Church Hall.

Left to right: Michael Frary, Deputy Harbour Master; Robert Smith, Harbour Master; Louise Allen, Harbour Administrator and Liz Blake, Admin. Assistant.

The Harbour Office

The Harbour Master at Wells and his team are responsible for navigation in an area reaching two miles to the north of the Fairway buoy, Holkham Church to the west and Stiffkey outfall pipe to the east, as well as all matters concerning the quayside and harbour area.

There are ten Harbour Commissioners, each appointed for three years, with an option to be co-opted for a further three years after which they must stand down. When a post is due to become vacant, a notice is published asking for applications from persons living within a ten-mile radius of Wells to fill the vacancy and following interviews, the most suitable person is appointed.

The Harbour Office was built in 1869 as a lifeboat house but in 1896 was bought by the Parish Council and in 1897 became the Jubilee Tea Rooms to commemorate Queen Victoria's diamond jubilee. In 1908, the rear part housed the horse-drawn fire engine and, during the second world war, was taken over by the Home Guard. From 1990 to 2004 it was divided into two sections to serve as the Harbour Office and Maritime Museum and in 2004 was completely refurbished and is now used entirely as a Harbour Office.

National Coastwatch Institution

Coastwatch is a charitable organisation with 42 stations. The Wells station was opened in 2006 and is staffed by volunteers following the withdrawal of government funding to the coastguards who manned it formerly.

Volunteers are trained and the station is assessed to reach Declared Facility Status, achieved in 2008, enabling it to work with search & rescue helicopters, coastguards, RNLI, and police.

It is built 55 feet above sea level, giving an 8-mile view to the horizon. It is equipped to plot the positions of ships. Incidents may be be reported to Yarmouth Coastguards who are authorised to contact the RNLI if it is decided that lifeboats are needed.
In winter the station is manned from 9 am to 4 pm and in summer from 8 am to 6 pm except in June, July and August when it is manned from 8 am to 8 pm.

John Blakeley (left) and Peter Bowles (above)

HM Coastguard

The coastguards meet on a Tuesday evening at their station in Bases Lane in Wells for training.

The picture shows Tony Garbutt, sector manager for North Norfolk (centre) with Steve Willshire, Station Officer, on his right, together with some of the Coastguard rescue officers.

Wells Lifeboat

These photographs show the current Wells lifeboat being launched as part of a regular training drill exercise. The *Doris M Mann of Ampthill* is a Mersey class lifeboat named after a generous benefactor. She has been in operation since 1990.

Above: Members of the lifeboat crew including four former coxswains. (left to right) Graham Walker, Sonny Warner, Tony Jordan, David Cox and Allen Frary.

Right: The inflatable inshore lifeboat *Jane Ann III* is pictured being launched as part of the same exercise.

Children's Day at the Lifeboat Station. Every Wednesday evening during the summer holidays, the Lifeboat Station is open to children, who enjoy role-playing as lifeboatmen, complete with all the gear.

The Fire Service

These photos show the Wells Fire Team led by Doug (Spud) Kelly
at one of their Wednesday evening practice drills. The Fire Station
moved to its new site just out of town in 1965. It was previously in
the building next to the library. The fire-fighters are all part-timers
and are summoned to call outs via a paging system.

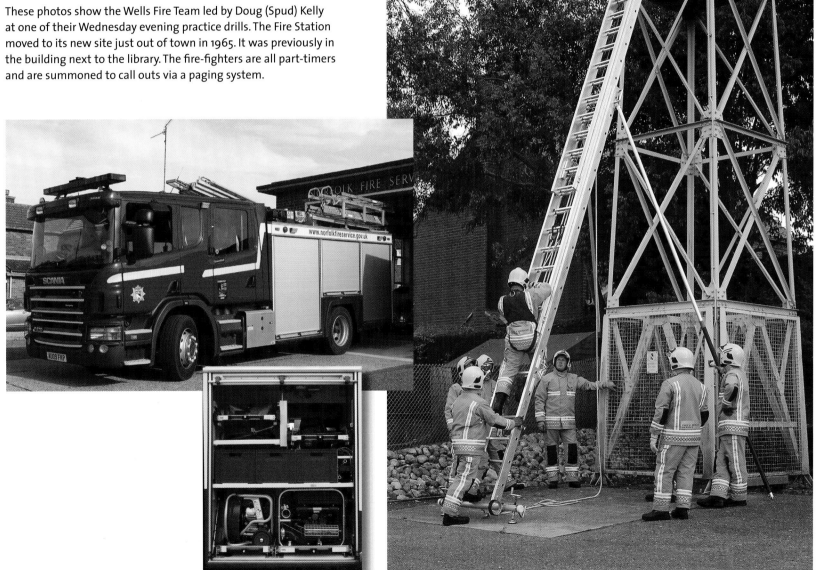

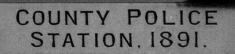

The Police

The new Police Station stands in Polka Road, replacing the original building on Church Plain.

Left to right: PC Jason Pegden, PCSO Cassie Doubleday, PC Simon Blakeley & Inspector Mike Brown.

The House that Moved

May Savidge lived in a fifteenth-century house in Hertfordshire for many years. She had lovingly spent time and money on renovating the house when, in 1953, she was informed that the local council had decided to demolish it to make way for a new roundabout. She fought the decision for sixteen years before accepting the inevitable.

However, before the demolition team moved in, she persuaded the council to let her take the house away and to re-erect it on another site. May chose Wells and all the components of the house – bricks, beams and windows were carefully numbered and their positions recorded in a notebook. A plot of land, formerly the ropewalk garden, was bought and the house was moved to Wells in 1970 loaded on eleven lorries.

For ten years, May lived in a small caravan without electricity and with water coming from a standpipe, while she pressed on with the work. She eventually moved into the house at the age of seventy, but there was still much work to be done. May died in 1993 aged 82 and the restoration work was taken over by Christine Adams, her niece, who moved into something resembling a shell; walls and a roof and little else. The house is now complete and is used as a bed & breakfast guest house. .

The marathon efforts and sheer determination of May Savidge have been turned into a book.

May Savidge at work (above)
and Christine Adams (left).

IN MEMORY OF

WILLIAM T. ANNISON.	GEORGE F. E. SMITH.		ARTHUR J. RINGER.
VICTOR G. BAKER.	GEORGE DYE.	GEORGE D. LACK.	WALTER G. RIX.
GEORGE BARNES.	JOHN W. DYE.	HENRY LACK.	HERBERT W. SEAMAN.
LIONEL A. BELL.	RICHARD FRANCIS.	ROBERT J. LACK.	WALTER H. SEAMAN.
ALFRED P. BONE.	FRANK FROST.	EDWARD W. LAXTON.	JOHN SHAUL.
HARRY BONE.	HENRY FROST.	WILLIAM H. LEGGETT.	HERBERT W. SIZELAND.
JOHN BRIDGES.	ARTHUR C. GENT.	OSMAN E. B. LLOYD.	ALBERT J. SKEET.
A. PERCY BUNTING.	PERCY E. GREEN.	ALFRED G. LONG.	ALBERT W. SKINNER.
BEN J. BUSBY.	WILFRED J. GROOM.	JAMES W. LONG.	ROBERT J. SMITH.
ERNEST BUSSEY.	WALTER GROOM.	HERBERT W. LOYNES.	EDWARD F. SOUTHGATE.
FREDERICK BYCROFT.	ARTHUR J. GRUMMETT.	HECTOR C. MARGETTS.	FRANCIS R. TAYLOR.
ALFRED G. CALTHROP.	HERBERT W. HAMMOND.	JOHN MUSSETT.	JOHN WALLER.
VICTOR J. COOK.	HERBERT HARRIS.	AHIJAH A. NEWMAN.	ROBERT WARREN.
ALFRED CREED.	ERNEST R. HAWES.	ERNEST A. NEWMAN.	CHARLES W. WELLS.
GEORGE CUBITT.	SAM HENDRY.	GEORGE F. PRATT.	EDWARD W. WOODHOUSE.
BENNIE T. DAWES.	RICHARD HIBBERT.	EDWARD J. RAISBURY.	FRANCIS W. WOODROW.
GEORGE E. DAWS.	ALBERT HINSON.	ALBERT R. REDDING.	RICHARD WOODROW.
WILLIAM C. DAWS.	NELSON HINSON.	FREDERICK W. REDDING.	CHARLES W. WRIGHT.
ALFRED DURHAM.	ALFRED W. LACK.	ARTHUR P. REEVE.	PHILIP YOUNGMAN.

WHO FELL IN THE GREAT WAR 1914-1918.

1939 – 1945

CHARLES E. ABLE.	HERBERT COE.	ERNEST O. HOLMAN.	HAROLD MITSON.
JOSIAH C. BARNES.	WILLIAM DOYLE.	CHARLES JORDAN.	THEODORE NEILSEN.
KENNETH BARRETT.	HARRY ECCBEER.	WALTER JORDAN.	CHARLES E. NORMAN.
NORMAN BARRETT.	RAYMOND ELLENDER.	TREVOR KING.	HERBERT NUDDS.
KEITH BOND.	LEONARD W. FARROW.	ADRIAN LAWS.	LEONARD C. PAGE.
CHARLES BUTTERS.	JOHN GOLDING.	FREDERICK LACK.	NOEL SPALDING.
LEONARD CALVER.	GEORGE GRIMES.	RICHARD LAKE.	ALBERT SAUNDERS.
LESLIE CADAMY.	STEPHEN E. HOWELL.	GEORGE R. LOVICK.	ARCHIE THOMPSON.
ALFRED WATERSON.		JOHN RIPPON WILLIAMS.	

LEST WE FORGET

WE SHALL REMEMBER THEM

The War Memorial

The War Memorial at the end of Clubbs Lane is dedicated to those from Wells killed in the two World Wars.
Fresh flowers are put in place every Friday by the Women's Branch of the British Legion.

The Old Custom House

The seventeenth-century Old Custom House is one of the town's oldest buildings. Customs revenues were collected in Wells from 1676 until 1881 when, due to the decline in shipping, collection was moved to King's Lynn.

Peter Rainsford and his wife Maddie bought the house in 1983 and restored it, while running Standard Chandlery on East Quay. Now a B&B, the house's history, with its proximity to the quay, make it popular with visitors.

Peter has been very active in local organisations, including the successful campaign to keep the Cottage Hospital open; Homes for Wells, a scheme for buying houses which might otherwise become holiday homes to let to people with local connections; and Chairman of the Wells Business Forum.

In 1993, Peter joined the Wells Lifeboat as Deputy Launching Authority and was also behind the town magazine, *The Quay*, which incorporates all the church and town news.

Standard Chandlery is now run by John Crook.

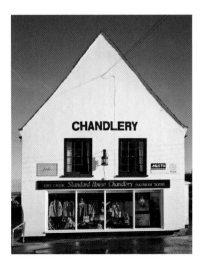

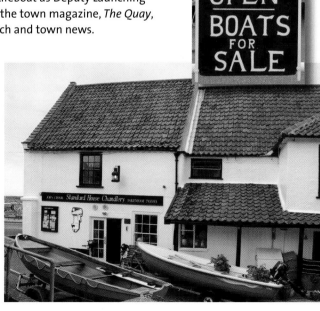

The East End

The east end of the town was where the fishermen and their families used to live. Some of the small alleyways and cottages remain, but many have been demolished or have become second homes and are used as holiday homes. This was the old ship-building area of the town.

JOLLY SAILOR YARD

Wells Sailing Club

Sailing and windsurfing are popular pursuits during the summer. Wells has an active sailing club founded in 1913 which holds an annual Regatta during the August Bank Holiday.

The 12-Square-Metre Sharpie has traditionally been the strongest fleet (right). Built mainly in the 1930s these elegant craft became popular in Wells in the 1940s and early 50s. Wells has provided many European and British Champions in this class.

Wells Town FC

The club started in 1905, playing on a number of fields before settling at Beach Road. They began at Mill Farm, moved to Market Lane and even played at Stiffkey after the 1978 floods damaged the beach bank.

WELLS TOWN F.C.
THE HOME OF THE SEASIDERS

In 1996 the clubhouse was built with a lottery grant and the same year the first team won the Junior Cup in an exciting final at Carrow Road, Norwich.

There are two adult teams but youth teams are encouraged and coached. The club has several local sponsors: Hodgkinson Builders (Midland) Ltd; Leftleys; Pop in; Wells Harbour Railway and Just Wells Holidays Ltd.

Bowls, Croquet and Tennis

The Bowls Club was originally based in the garden of Bishop Ingle house. The original clubhouse dating from 1934 was updated and renovated in 1988 with the help of Lottery Funding. The club enters several leagues and competitions during the season and a new petanque court adds to the facilities available.

Tennis and bowls are also played at the nearby Elsmith Bowls Club.

WELLS TOWN BOWLS AND PETANQUE CLUB

BOWLS SHOES MUST BE WORN

The King's Morris

Since their formation back in 1978, the King's Morris have become a regular attraction, nay, institution, around the pubs and villages of North Norfolk. They are to be found every year performing on the Buttlands or on the Quay and refreshing themselves in the *Albatros* afterwards. They are ably led by the longest serving member of the team, 'Squire', Ian Price, while David 'lamb chops' Jackson is the most photographed member of the team, and Ian Heighton the proud owner of one of the largest tankards ever seen in regular use – a huge half gallon capacity. They are occasionally joined by Norman the Konkerer and the pet Dragon, Izeels (as in 'Draggin' 'is 'eels')!

Wheels-next-the-Sea

Started in 2009 and fast becoming a popular annual June event, Wheels-next-the-sea attracts more than 500 bikes to the Beach Road playing field and raises funds for the Wells Scouts. Bikes and bikers come in all shapes and sizes from vintage to veteran, and there is always a good turnout of the popular Gold Wing machines. This is an enjoyable day out with plenty of enthusiastic discussion on the finer points of the bikes on show.

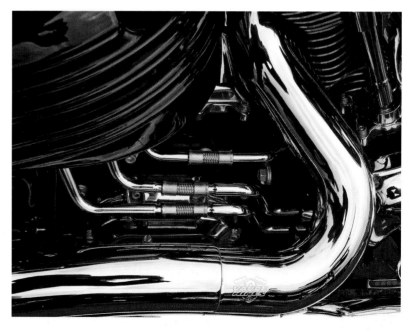

Wells Carnival

Wells Carnival is an action packed week popular with young and old, residents and visitors alike. A tremendous amount of work is put in by the Carnival Committee to ensure a successful event that raises money for local charities. The week culminates in the parade from the Buttlands to the Quay.

119

Raft Race

The raft race held in 2009 was the first after a break of several years. It proved to be so popular that it was decided to hold it again during carnival week but over a slightly shorter course. This has resulted in an increased number of entries with some very imaginative craft and most paddlers manage to get themselves very wet.

The Frarys

Frary's shellfish stall was started by Dennis Frary in 1957, selling shellfish from the back of a van on the Quay near the Harbour Office. Dennis's sons, Martin and Andy took over the family business in 1994 and moved to the present stall on the Quayside, where they sell crabs and lobsters caught from their own boat *Arandora Star*. The stall is run by Andy and Martin's wives, Jane and Pam, and sells a wide range of shellfish and wet fish.

ALL
CRABS & LOBSTERS
CAUGHT BY OUR OWN
BOAT
ARANDORA STAR

A & M. FRARY
CRAB & LOBSTER FISHERMEN

A & M. FRARY
EST. 1957
Shellfish Caught

Pamela, Jane and Andy Frary

Mandy Frary dressing crabs

Dennis Frary

Big Blue Sky

Big Blue Sky was founded in 2000 on the site of a former garage on the Warham Road just out of town. Its owner, Catherine Edgington, a former primary school teacher and garden designer, runs a bright, colourful and airy shop 'where everything comes from Norfolk'. Big Blue Sky won the 2009 *Daily Telegraph* award for Best Local, Homes & Interiors Shops.

128

Sue Fisher and Sara Philips outside the shop on the Quay.

The Natural Soap Company

Sara Phillips started the Natural Soap Company in her kitchen about thirteen years ago. The enterprise snowballed and, by advertising online, she now has customers all over the world. The manufacturing process is in an industrial unit where she employs four other workers.

Since 2008, Sara has been editing the Wells magazine *The Quay* following the death of the original editor, Bernard Phillips.

Edna Eaglen wrapping soap and Gail Whitworth filling pots with bubble bath.

Wells Deli

Wells Deli on the Quay is a popular stopping off place for a coffee and snack.

The Real Ale Shop, Branthill

The Real Ale Shop was Teddy Maufe's idea for diversification at Branthill Farm, where his family has farmed for more than 70 years. Five years ago, eight Norfolk brewers were represented; now the number is fifteen.

In co-operation with Woodforde's brewery in Woodbastwick and the Iceni Brewery in Mundford, Teddy has worked to promote the link between high quality locally grown malting barley, especially the fine Maris Otter variety, and the finished pint. Growing enthusiasm for good local produce has helped the business to success.

Whin Hill Cider, Stearman's Yard

Peter Lynn and Jim Ferguson began producing Whin Hill Cider in a Wells garage in 1994 using apples which had been brought in. In the same year they planted an orchard where they now have 2000 trees, of which 1300 are cider apples, 500 are apples for apple juice and the rest are pears for perry. Pruning the trees takes the whole of January.

At Easter, and for the whole of the summer, Stearman's Yard in Wells is open to the public.

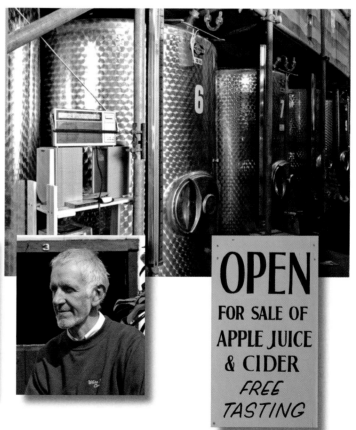

Catherine Temple
Mrs Temple's Cheese

Catherine Temple, born into a farming family, moved to Wells and started cheese making commercially in 2002. She specialises in local brands, such as the hard 'Walsingham' cheese, the soft blue veined 'Binham Blue' and the Gouda-like 'Warham'. The farm at Wighton produces eleven cheeses from their cows.

The Temples are also proud of their ecologically friendly process which converts waste products into methane gas which in turn is used to produce electricity, supplying not only the farm but also feeding into the National Grid.

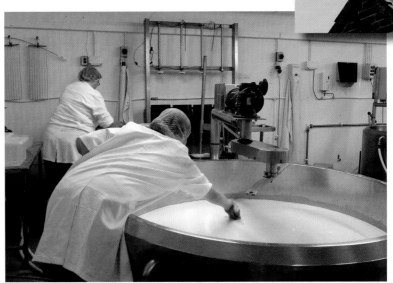

James Case
Boat builder

James Case learned his trade in the 1970s working at several of Norfolk's boat building yards during his apprenticeship. James eventually set up his own business in an old barn in Wells, previously used for storing boats. Very quickly work began to find him. He has never needed to do any advertising and is lucky enough to have more work than he can handle. This, and working alone, suits him well and enables him to ensure that what goes out of the yard has his stamp of quality on it.

JAMES CASE
BOATBUILDER
TIMBER & G.R.P. REPAIRS
MAINTENANCE
RESTORATION ~ RE~FITS
CARPENTRY ~ JOINERY
TEL:(01328) 710550
MOBILE   07887 594167

The Beach

The beach can sometimes be deserted, as these pictures show.

In winter the wide open spaces attract walkers (and dogs) – the couple of miles to Holkham and back can be a cure for most of life's troubles. Longer walks are also available for the enthusiast.

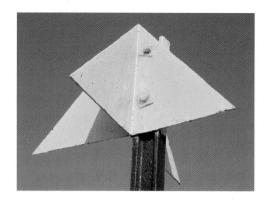

Beach Huts

There are more than 200 beach huts at Wells, famously captured in Lorrie Tallis' photograph which forms the end papers of this book. Some shown here were made by James Ward (below), a Fakenham based carpenter specialising in beach huts. As well as traditional beach locations, many of James' huts are bought for gardens throughout the country as offices, studios and summerhouses. James has his own website www.uk-beachhuts.co.uk.

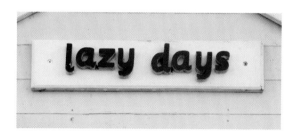

Danger
Underwater structure

No swimming near groynes

NO LIFEGUARDS

SWIM AT OWN RISK

No Fire

On The Beach

No Dogs

Beyond This Point

WARNING

THESE WATERS ARE TIDAL
IT IS EXTREMELY DANGEROUS
TO BE CAUGHT ON THE
FAR SIDE OF THE CHANNEL
BY THE INCOMING TIDE.
WHEN THE TIDE BEGINS
TO FLOW

IN AN EMERGENCY
DIAL 999
AND ASK FOR THE
COASTGUARD

GRID REFERENCE:

DO NOT INTERFERE WITH THIS
EQUIPMENT – THE LIFE IT
SAVES COULD BE
YOURS!

Typical of the current day and age,
these signs list the "Don't Do's"!

Here is one of the "Must Do's" – the annual sand castle
competition always attracts a large crowd to the beach in August.

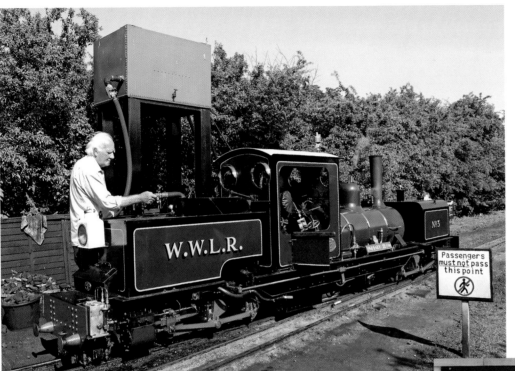

WELCOME TO THE WELLS AND
WALSINGHAM LIGHT RAILWAY
THE LONGEST 10¼ GAUGE RAILWAY
IN THE WORLD

ADULT RETURN	£8·00
ADULT SINGLE	£6·50
CHILD RETURN	£6·50
CHILD SINGLE	£5·00

CHILDREN UNDER FOUR FREE   FOUR TO FOURTEEN CHILD FARES

The Wells Walsingham Railway

The Wells to Walsingham railway was the brainchild of Lt Commander Roy Francis (above, filling the engine water tank) who spent three years in laying track and installing the railway infrastructure, such as refreshment and car parking areas, toilets and engine maintenance sheds.

Opened in 1982, the train runs for the thirty minute, four mile journey between Wells and Walsingham.

The station name of 'Wells on Sea' was shortened by the railway company from Wells-next-the Sea to save space on signs and timetables.

There is one steam engine, 'The Norfolk Hero', soon to be joined by another currently under construction, and two diesel engines.

Driver Ian Williams (above) and Lorrie Tallis (above right).

Holkham

Holkham Hall from the south. Holkham Hall is the cornerstone of the Holkham Estate which covers 25,000 acres and includes the Pinewoods Caravan Park, The Victoria Hotel and The Globe Inn. Ancestral seat of the Earls of Leicester, the Hall was built in the Palladian style of architecture and completed in 1764 after the death of the first Earl.

The Thomas Willliam Coke monument (above) was built by subscription in 1845. The ice house (left) provided an essential function before the days of modern refrigeration.

Lesley Clarke, guide at Holkham Hall,
on duty in the old kitchen.

Holkham Country Fair

Holkham Country Fair is held every two years. Set against the magnificent
background of Holkham Hall, it attracts more than 45,000 visitors over two days.

Pinewoods Holiday Park

Pinewoods Holiday Park, part of the Holkham Estate, has developed significantly since the early 1960s when a few small tents and caravans were scattered around an almost empty field. There are now spaces for more than 600 static and 400 touring caravans.

Right: Ian Curtis driving holidaymakers along Beach Road.

Wells Harbour Railway

This miniature 10.25-inch-gauge railway opened in 1996. It carries passengers the one-mile journey between Harbour Station and Pinewoods Holiday Park.

The pinewoods were planted in the 1870s to consolidate the dunes protecting marshland reclaimed from the sea.

Norfolk is famous for its sunsets. This one is taken from Two Furlong Hill looking over towards Holkham.

Bibliography

A Dream of the Land – John Hansell
The Inns and Public Houses of Wells-next-the-Sea –
    Mike Welland (in preparation)
East Anglia – Hammond Innes
East Anglia Villages – John Potter
East Anglia Panoramas – John Potter
Essentially English – Patrick Ward
Elements of the North Norfolk Coast – David North &
    Martin Hayward-Smith
Wells-next-the-Sea East End Walk – Wells Local History Group
Wells-next-the-Sea West End Walk – Wells Local History Group
Wells-next-the-Sea – Sketchbook – Wells Local History Group
Wells-next-the-Sea Lifeboat – A History
Wells-next-the-Sea – Millennium Project (in Wells Library)

Acknowledgements

Christine Adams; Hazel Ashley; Ton Brouwer; Inspector Mike Brown and the police in Wells; James Case; Lesley Clarke; Jean Court; David Cox; Catherine Edgington; Graham Green; Nicky King; Ian Heighton and The King's Morris; Steve Finch; Lt. Commander Francis; Andy & Martin Frary and their families; Doug Kelly and the fire fighters; Gwyneth Hall; Peter Lynn and Jim Ferguson; Teddy Maufe; Terry Norton; Sara Philips and the employees at Natural Soap; Peter & Maddie Rainsford; Suzanne Rands; Gail Robins; Peter Scillitoe; Ian Scott for permission to use the gantry; Robert Smith and the team at the Harbour Office; Peter & Jean Terrington; Catherine Temple; Ian Williams; Steve Willshire & Tony Garbutt; Dennis Woods and the Coast Watch volunteers; Julia Rafferty at Wells Library & Learning Centre and our fellow students; Mike Welland for generously giving his time, advice and expert knowledge of Wells through the years, and for allowing us access to his unpublished book on the pubs of Wells.

Dick Malt – for another excellent book design!

The Authors

Janet Angles was born in London and moved to Norfolk in 1961. She has always been interested in anything creative and at various times has taught art, craft and needlework, before developing a passion for digital photography. After attending a beginners' course at Wells Library in 2004 she carried on to complete the NCFE level 3 in 2009. She has two daughters and four grandchildren.

John Warham was born in Lancashire, brought up in Yorkshire and spent most of his working life in various countries in Asia, before moving back to the UK and settling in Thornham in 2000. He is married to Sue and they have two grown-up children, Paul and Jane.

Photographic Notes

Except where stated, all the photographs in this book were taken by John Warham and Janet Angles between 2009-2010. John uses Canon 450D and 50D digital camera bodies with Canon EF 70-300mm DO IS USM, Canon 18-55mm and Sigma 10-20mm zoom lenses. Janet uses a Panasonic Lumix DMC-G1K camera with Panasonic 14-45 mm/F3.5-5.6 ASPH/MEGA OIS lens and Panasonic 45-200 mm/F4.0-5.6 MEGA OIS lens. Also, on occasion, a Hoya UV filter. The photographs were processed in either Elements 6 or Photoshop CS4.

Wells - next - the - Sea

No's 101 - 119

No's 120 - 168

No's 169 - 207